ONTOLOGY
OF
BLUE

ONTOLOGY OF BLUE

DAVID BELLUSCI

Seraphim
EDITIONS

Copyright © 2016 David Bellusci

All rights reserved. No part of this publication may be reproduced or transmitted in any form or by any means – electronic or mechanical, including photocopying, recording or any information storage or retrieval system – without written permission from the publisher, except by a reviewer who wishes to quote brief passages for inclusion in a review.

The publisher gratefully acknowledges the financial assistance of the Canada Council for the Arts and the Ontario Arts Council.

Canada Council for the Arts / Conseil des arts du Canada

ONTARIO ARTS COUNCIL
CONSEIL DES ARTS DE L'ONTARIO
an Ontario government agency
un organisme du gouvernement de l'Ontario

Library and Archives Canada Cataloguing in Publication

Bellusci, David Christian, 1960-, author
    Ontology of blue / David Bellusci.

Poems.
ISBN 978-1-927079-44-7 (paperback)

    I. Title.

PS8603.E47O58 2016   C811'.6   C2016-904270-7

Editor: Robert Priest
Design and Typography: Rolf Busch

Published in 2016 by
Seraphim Editions
4456 Park Street
Niagara Falls, ON
L2E 2P6

Printed and bound in Canada

Acknowledgements

I met Pier Giorgio Di Cicco in the Winter of 2004 while he was Visiting Lecturer at the University of Toronto. He took the time to listen to my many "poetry issues." Pier Giorgio has been an unquestionable source of inspiration for me – and poetry mentor.

Francesca L'Orfano whom I met in Halifax in 2003 at the Canadian Society for Italian Studies congress was instrumental in my decision to publish poetry. Francesca, an artist herself, reminded me that "art is meant to be communicated."

Allison Adelle Hedge Coke, Teri Grimm and Lee Ann Roripaugh at the University of Nebraska, provided me with constructive feedback on my poetry over the years as I experimented with different poetic styles. I thank them for encouraging me to publish.

The Association of Italian-Canadian Writers has been a creative point of reference for me – the AICW has been an excellent forum to exchange ideas.

I wish to thank Maureen Whyte and Seraphim Editions for publishing my first volume of existential poetry. Working with Maureen has been a wonderful experience.

This volume of poetry has also been inspired by nuns, priests and the poor whom I have met during my studies, travels and teaching.

If it's possible to thank "nature," then, a word of thanks to winter, the most beautiful season, thanks to the rain, snow, ice and silence. A special mention of the Luskville chalet on the Ottawa River where many of these poems were written, especially during the winter months when silence freezes. I continue to ask questions about what I believe, how I live, where I am going, and how I can help.

I am grateful to my family and friends, for their role in my life, and who have been a source of inspiration in my poetry. A special thanks to my sister, Maria, who has been my closest friend since childhood.

This work is dedicated to my mother, †Rosa Montagano Bellusci and my father, †Nicola Bellusci; my parents have always been and still are a fundamental part of my life.

A word is not yet on my tongue,
before you,
Yahweh, know all about it. (Ps. 139)

CONTENTS

Acknowledgements   5

Section 1 – Remembering Caravaggio

Flesh songs	14
Sorbonne	15
Touch	16
Drawing	17
Serpent's coil	18
1920s Berlin Gästehaus (after the Wall)	19
Lady Anne Clifford	20
Quirinale Gardens	21
Filippo and Esther	22
Caravaggio's heads	23
Plato's Florence	24
Oak borders	25
Turner's colour	27
Village paint	28
Arrivederci	29
River dreams	30

Section 2 – Constellation silence

Silent harp	32
Ripples	33
Shells	34
Poem by the river	35
Locks	36
Lavender mist	37
Iron bridge	38
Cracking steps	39
Copernicus	40
Frozen satin	41
Ice shack	42
Play house	43
Nebraska homestead	44
6 a.m.	46
Dusk	47
Third Sunday in March	48
Spring	49
Buttery grapes	50
Time	51

Section 3 – Mango Season

Cali	54
After-school downpour	55
Only in Bogota	56
Free coffee	58
Broken bed	60
Santa Marta	62

Installing the President	64
Bombin hat	65
Doña Marcela	66
Luna Azúl	69
Oaxáca's grasshoppers	70
Man in the pick-up	71
Tea in secret	72
Beauty's Restaurant	73
Guerrillas	75
Nigerian dream	77
Visit	78
Listen!	80
Monsoon petals	82
Cocunut chutney	83
Double-burger avenue	84
Christmas in Chicago	85
American connections	86
Arrivals	88
Airport shuttle	89

Section 4 – Mosaics Made in Italy

Summer breeze in southern Italy	92
Mamma's home	93
Stranger in a village	95
Halifax, 1955	97
Afternoon tuna	98
Blue harbour	100
Cappuccini	102
Tiramisù	104

Sicilian cannoli	105
Lost in the city	106
Feeling guilty	107
Jumpity-Jump	108
Papa's watch	110
Relics	112
Fontanta di Trevi	113
Silence of the Tiber	114
Roman torches	115
Capes and hoods	116
Murano	117
Venice on a Monday	118

Section 5 – Purple fountains

Montreal diner	122
Cutting me	123
Table for one	124
Unknown	125
G.M. Hopkins on Friendship	126
Unshaven	127
Broken leash	129
She	130
Two transfer	131
Pretty woman	132
Phone call	133
On the floor	134
Portuguese dance	136
Sleeping with Malebranche	137
Mornings in France	138

Morning hymn	140
The End ...	141
November leaves	142
Plastic daffodils	143
Alone	144
Gold box	145
Bruno	146
A Nun's Veil	147
She stands	148
Standing in bronze	149
Chant	150
Incense	152
Dedicated to a novice	153

SECTION 1

Remembering Caravaggio

ONTOLOGY OF BLUE

Flesh songs

>The boy holds a wooden flute
>to his thick lips,
>fingers feeling holes,
>head covered in a brown and blue hood.
>A caged parrot, a malicious owl.
>Lilies in a vase,
>withered flowers.
>A snuffed out candle, signs
>of smoke. Papers strewn, her glasses
>on her nose, grandma holds
>music sheets.
>Her daughter reveals a fleshy
>neckline, a glass of wine, tilted,
>cheekbones red, singing.
>Blonde boy toys his mouth,
>the collie licks grapes. Grandpa,
>triple-chinned, grabs his frothy beer,
>gold Belgian.
>Shiny lemon wedges curled,
>sliced fish stretching in a tray,
>bread rolls, and oranges.
>A rabbit. Something Flemish.

Sorbonne

She walks barefoot, her
beaded anklet wrapped,
loose. A mini-skirt, light blue
cotton, red rose prints, her
bohemian freedom. I have a
picture of you drinking a carton
of strawberry milk.

You, me, feeling the warmth
of our hands, gently held,
the scented breeze,
the Eiffel Tower looks over us.

Paris, lighting our evening walks,
lilacs of your body.

A party at her place, they passed
colombian joints. I watched,
one by one.

Louise – they carried to the Renault.
Morning cars hooting, waking me up.
I dreamed the "au revoir" train
tracks.

You told me in a letter we live in
two galaxies, me and you.

I still wear her Sorbonne sweat shirt.

Touch

>Warmth trickles through his palm,
>his blood; he wants to touch
>the horse's long eyelashes. Instead,
>he plucks the fruit, hanging over,
>and sucks on sweetness. He stands
>lonely, senses fatigue sedating his
>mind, paralysing each limb of his body,
>not finishing the succulent juices, he
>drops in dizziness.
>
>Her eyes settle on his thick wavy hair,
>then his deep eyes, full wet lips,
>body like hers, different, but not like
>the animal beside him. She steps closer,
>silently, as though not to wake him. She
>puts her hands gently on his chest,
>kisses his face, moist lips, she feels
>warmth of his breath. A tickling sensation
>fills her body.
>
>His eyes open to meet her.

DAVID BELLUSCI

Drawing*

A creation of Marie-Pierre,
or God, flesh detailed lines.

Lying, fully extended, a restful pose.

Your eyes turned away, tracing
a Roman nose. Lips concealed,
thick neck.

A god yourself. Maybe.

Muscles define your long arms,
athlete thighs. Legs smooth, your
feet solid.

Your body pulsates
before me; every bone a purpose.

Hundreds of sketches
discarded sheets

to produce the perfect man.

---

* *National Art Gallery, Ottawa.*
  Exhibition of French Artists in Rome.

Serpent's coil

around hard brown bark
she grabs the swollen tail
fruit
in death's hand
deadly bite
firm red lips, strong chin
forehead straight
corner of her eyes mock
death's ugliness
thin fingers caress the fruit
tight in her right hand
smooth scales
blue squares and black diamonds
inch
hypnotise seduce
her reaching touch
– just once:
to taste your sweet poison.

DAVID BELLUSCI

1920s Berlin Gästehaus (after the Wall)

Her heels cut my thoughts,
I waited for Hacker-Pschoor.

Hard oak tables square and straight.

Fried sausages, after classes.
For her, Chilean wine, not too dry.

Beethoven hits his keys hard.

Parisian student Geneviève,
lectured me on international law.

Syllables brushed smooth on silk.

A *kleine* German lamp spies on us,
her rounded lips, my empty glass.

Summer *Strassen* of secret blues.

Broken Italian lyrics fall,
like ice in her hand, unmelted.

August ends. Again a train.

ONTOLOGY OF BLUE

Lady Anne Clifford

    Your milk-like skin,
        let me touch you.

    Your fresh fair face,
        softly your heart beats.

    Your neckline of lace,
    white blouse of silk,
        my fingers run through.

    Your feminine beauty,
        I revere.

    Your Yorkshire embraced –
    pearl bracelet
        for me to catch.

    Your pink ribbons from your finger
    to your breasts…
        may I untie them?

    Your blue eyes, perhaps Irish,
    daughter of an English Lord,
        my caresses kiss you.

    But you're married to Lord Mahoney:

    you embody his inheritance.

        Pierre Subleyras dreams,
        and I.

DAVID BELLUSCI

Quirinale Gardens

I stumbled across the gardens,
*French Artists in Rome, 17th-18th
Centuries*, Exhibition.

Yellow shades, Roman
sun, "Giardini Quirinale." Semi-
circular steps, cascade majestic.
A man in a formal suit, a woman,
ruffled layers, together, small, below
arching green trees.

A hard warm bench,
their whispers, Italian syllables,
carried by sparrows, lyrics of
Virgil's nightingale, nesting
on Vittoriano lamps.
Pointers and Lagottos race, snarling
in the dewy grass. A marble fountain
cools the morning air, water flows,
my throat dry. A Cane Corso joins
the competition, fenced by a stone
baluster, to a halt.

Wrens pipe loudest, covering lovers.

ONTOLOGY OF BLUE

Filippo and Esther

She folds her dress above
the right knee, as if uncertain.
Pointing with the other: *I am not
your goddess,* and *I know
what must be done.*

Bloody bodies torn, shredded
one by one, son after son. Unseen
in a pastel turquoise
sky serene, blue silk,
layers of gold and green
velvet, hide
royal red blood.

Esther's wide black eyes,
her open mouth and red tongue,
the shrilling syllables, a dry scream,
her ten slaughtered sons.

Caravaggio's heads

Blue silk dress her destiny layered white
soft shoulders, feminine flesh,
iron sword clenched tight hard
red hands determined veins.
White shirt creased in his blood, Judith's
bulging eyes devour Holofernes,
holds him like a lioness mauling her
agonising prey.

A ruddy teenager disheveled,
stares at me satisfied,
huge bearded head held,
adolescent hand, clenched fist,
stringy brute's hair falls.

Salomé smiles delighted, platter
of blood dripping, goat-like.
I want to touch his sun-beaten flesh,
eyes closed. Herodias stares.
Prize. Oath. Plot.
Capricious triangle.

Plato's Florence

>Melted turquoise – poured
>hazelnut pecan-chopped
>look!

>Glass bubbling fountains,
>red satin flutters in a piazza.

>Venus in her white
>shell.

>   David
>holds a sling, fist tight,
>bulging veins.

>New lip-stick, cherry-purple,
>wet thick
>hair falls to her hips
>   … pulled to one side.

>Roman sandals,
>American jeans,
>Moses reveals his horns.

>She rips the pomegranate
>– sucks the crimson juice.

>Reddened tongue,

>the *Symposium* opens.

Oak borders

    Naked flesh, muscled chests,
        black hair
curved thighs, pressing grass,
    – rocks.

Anvil.

Hammered, steady,
Aeolus labours tightened arms
    … bulging …

Bellows.

White horse, thick neck,
staring straight,
        eyes intense.

    Hair braided,
    he looks down,
riding – trotting, galloping,
    in red.

She holds a baby.
He gazes in love.

Vulcan stretching out
    brings flames.

Giraffes.

Crossed-wood columns,
– a frame ... a home ...

Four workers assemble
wooden layers. Poles fastened.

    ... turquoise shore,

Piero di Cosimo
plays the mandolin.

Turner's colours

Fading whites, blues
dissolve into foggy grey
branches.
Dark waves cover the crows,
endless song of hummingbird.
Powerful clouds move.
Turner takes me to the Thames,
Wordsworth, the Lake District,
painting green words on white
canvas. His thick brush
holds blue ink, plume. Feathers
cover lakeshore, young
shepherd attends to white flock.
It's Socrates who descends this hill
with a staff, a speech on words.
Only the cows listen.

ONTOLOGY OF BLUE

Village paint*

>Thoughts of Emily Carr
>West Coast firs, the Lillooet.
>Remote village shaded
>by thick pines
>dark skies.
>White Church, drums and hymns
>and Big Raven
>his deep eyes, thick black braids,
>reflecting:
>woman stands in deerskin dress,
>the baby warm on her back.
>River.
>Cold.
>Fire.
>Water separates villages, strange sounds,
>waves splash against granite rocks.
>Clouds skirt the sun in morning dance.
>Seagulls cry.
>Leafless trees, their red leaves,
>scattered, a mat.
>
>Swinging cot swings alone.

* *Vancouver Art Gallery, Emily Carr exhibition.*

DAVID BELLUSCI

Arrivederci

     June syllables, students abroad,
     railroad tracks meet in Berlin,
     friend points, body full, slim,
     French accent, in German she calls.
     My Italian, sweetened consonants,
     hands tight, I sang; flowers she picked.
     Beer foamed, dancing in Munich.
     Silence: Ode to Joy in a Gothic church.

     Her apartment close to St. Michel,
     she fed me Swiss cheese, baguettes, milk.
     Eiffel between us, fountains and lamplights.
     Turkish delights we tasted on the Seine,
     je t'aime, she writes, her hand like silk.
     Paris platform we waved. I never cried.

River dreams

I like it when you are far,
so I am forced to watch you,
to hear open syllables
because they are yours.
Like winter pine needles
I suck on them.

I like it when you are silent,
so I hear your breath, your
beat. Your wings
flutter, cover my naked body.
Leave me your feathers, to soar
into your silence.

I like it when you shout
my name,
hymns of water that pour
on a new-born.
The music of the rising sun
eyeing me.
Hide me in your eternal temple.

I like it when you are near,
so when the smell of you
turns me dizzy,
I taste your sacred presence,

consumed.

SECTION 2

Constellation silence

ONTOLOGY OF BLUE

Silent harp

Crisp, professional bond to start
my frozen hand, stuck syllables.
Plastic covers hard garden bulbs,
log cabin quivers on a hill dark.
Ceaseless knocks, walls falling apart,
that death dirge, eerie whispers call,
black heavens, tearless, hardened heart
put on Calliope's forgotten song.

A moon-lit stone path marks the door,
jacket, boots, dirty wet socks off.
The fire hisses, fingers unstuck, move.
The table is set, lips and tongue, raw.
Angelic flaps, feathers blue, mauve.
Her potion I drink, her whisper I yearn.

DAVID BELLUSCI

Ripples

Untouched sheets milky waves
liquid marks I suck,
the oak I brush into syllables,
not fingers, but spinning
somersaults of a wrung heart,
separated brains
before the orange ball returns.
No.
I wonder – the *awe* of awesome.
Greened hues, smoked pinks,
prism edges, Murano glass
trapped
in grey graphite, blue ink, laser black.
Leaves of mist whip me,
reddening my skin, cowhide rips
into me.
Arithmetic birds count the current,
I count their feathers, one by one.
And drip – piped cottage roof,
a tightened hose leaking.
Roof frame bleeds red, dressing
foggy arms, a peel of sun.
Ignored reeds inhale hummingbirds.
Small stones, last summer's ash,
there we buried the squirrel.

Shells

>... polished desert sands ...
>
>>... foamy oceans peak ...
>
>>>... your seaweed fingers ...

DAVID BELLUSCI

Poem by the river*

Sitting under oak canopy,
where the settlements began,
    totem, fleur-de-lis.
Listening, thunder, a warning.

Green-grey waves, stretch, separate
me from houses dotting the distant
shore.

Smooth canoes carved, chiselled,
bounce, tied to maple tree posts.

Anchoring ships, angry sails fight
wind, claiming river
howl in raging battle

rain spears   branches whip   leaves
forced   fall.

In their deerskin with bare
chests, Algonquin men eye

French women in black dresses
disembark, hidden in layers,
holy fabric.

Monseigneur waits.

**Trois-Rivières, Québec*

ONTOLOGY OF BLUE

Locks

        Muscles burst, twist, turn,
        cranks circle,
        solid iron lowers the draw-bridge,
        a moat, a castle, guarded
        turrets, graded steps,
        gates shut
        gates open,
        unloosened chains, passage secure.
        I light the cannon balls,
        fired arrows zigzag like fireflies.
        Helen signals, the trumpets blast,
        in helmet, maillot breast armour,
        she circles on the Pegasus,
        the enemy like vomiting drunks.
        She steals the sea, eyeing
        Paris' retreat.
        Possessed seas re-possessed.
        because Spartan dogs
        drink the profits.
        A statue of an Algonquin looks on.

Lavender mist

>Egret stands on a wire leg
>swallowing itself
>a distant silhouette.
>
>Seagulls caw-caw white
>ripples in water, clouds.
>Fish splash, frog?
>
>Fir trees drink shore
>tall grass feels marsh,
>pine branches lick
>without sound.
>
>Clouds puff, pinks orange,
>morning lavender mist.

Iron bridge

Sky a Gothic print,
narrow road, oncoming
lights … flicker past …
Trees in evening gowns flutter
layers of satin.
Routes, unknown
in dawn's morning strangeness.
Traces of a distant house, a single
lamp. No horses. No sheep.
A black gate.
Waters gush, chopping,
accompany me.
Dotted lights, silent cottages.
Road bends, uphill.
Clouds clear cautious light,
lining, a circle, directly
overhead.
Moon appears,
as if secretly unveiling
her prohibited body.
Clouds undress.
She displays herself,
Diana's spell.

Cracking steps*

Snow-caps taste cold, ice drips.
Porters packed, pans and all.
Grass – pebbles – rocks, a lost path
of paintings. Real Monet.

Clouds skirt the skies, voices cease,
breathing moves, the rocks I climb.
Leather boots, the Canadian kind gripping ankles,
jeans in blue nylon, a pole he carved for me.

Christopher, guiding lips,
our feathered creatures dance.
Snow caps disappear in stealing clouds.
Scarf. Hat. Coat. Gloves.

Cabin smoke, soup, coffee, a chocolate.
Frozen mattress, iced toes, reading *failure*
in graffiti. Cosmic midnight, Van Gogh's hour.
Gravity pulls, stars dizzy spell.

Spinning puke, yellow stuff out,
black-lined peaks, play toys.
Corpse in slow motion, I chug.

And kneel.

*Climbing Mount Kilimanjaro, Tanzania.

ONTOLOGY OF BLUE

Copernicus

>Ice-fishing shacks, frozen river,
>southeast Orion illuminates –
>transforms cosmic black
>widow, dead eggs. Flicker:
>Taurus and Perseus, webs apart.
>– wired blueness pointing south:
>Pisces framed, holes drilled deep
>make-shift home, crawling space:
>soldiers, monks, Uranus, Jupiter,
>Comet Halley's tail, intrudes …
>Cat whiskers, steps silent,
>hairy spiders hide, crawling stars:
>twilight red, south southwest, strings
>– wires fall, moose-skin warmth
>chimney smoke offered, planets.
>Leafless praying mantises kneel,
>mystics trance in starry ice,
>swallowing fish caught in bear
>paws, polar weight. Sagittarius
>sleepily waits:

DAVID BELLUSCI

Frozen satin

Yellow lights between black hills,
like a woman wearing her diamonds
on a satin dress.
Far away, across the river,
they dot the shore.
A mallard rides with her companion.
Sharp-cut jewels brighten,
she steps closer, unveiled,
icicles drip from her smooth
fingers.
Her white ankles sink
into shards of ice,
black hair,
covered in a Norwegian head scarf.
She licks the maple sap, her tongue
rough wet from sweet bark.
A flood
of geese fills her space, their calls
bruise her limbs,
breaking links, her crystals fall.
Cold sap runs on her white legs,
satin
layers form a black cushion,
she drags her head,
soaking, sucked into the earth's
frosty crust.

Ice shack

Faded green, middle of a river,
frozen, make-shift home.
Alone.
Fisherman breathes, warm
air piped.
Wind belts, northern frost
white crystal layers frozen
blankets protect.
Icy waters.
Grey clouds open
pinkish horizon lines
bushy evergreens.
Shack deathly quiet, unmoved.
Line secretly plunges drawing
silver fish.
Blue diamond butterfly hints
springtime message.
Bend. Catch.
Slapping windy night plays, dizzy
constellation spins.

DAVID BELLUSCI

Play house

      A toy construction soaked,
      shivers in mahogany logs
      layers of wood dripping fear,
      tears running down the sides.
      Winter rain targets the A-frame
      a mistaken punishment
      caught alone, winds blow hard
      holiday cabin, curtained windows
      I do not move.
      Covered head, hidden face, light struggles,
      Who's holding the candle? Is it you?
      In your toy-house seeking
      someone to play with.
      Frozen by zapping flashes
      fierce skies glare with a wrinkled
      angry forehead.

      The logger puts out his flame.

ONTOLOGY OF BLUE

Nebraska homestead

Wind howled. In a brick stone house,
she sat for Jesse rock'n back and forth,
the dying fire, and list'n'in, starin hard
out the window, watch'n darkness come.
Her eyes on that single spot,
the mantle, Kansas plate show'n a crack.
That damn annoy'n mark. He bought
the gift just after she turned eighteen.
They married up north.
The line turned black and needed work.
Soot from smoke and ash
a fav'rite piece of household furniture.
She feels her heart and beat'n hard,
a little darker purple sunset now.
She's wondrin' when he's gett'n back.
Stands up to check her little Josh,
and covers her darl'n fold'n him in blue
and white. A shawl she knit,
like Jesse asked before her little baby came.
He's sleep'n quiet. Mamma smiles.
Some boiled potatoes covered in a pot,
chicken cooked she slaughtered fast
at noon. Thought Jesse would be
home before sun set. He did say.
She thought she heard him gall'pi'n
in, the wind the sky are yell'n hard.
Her ears began to twitch.

DAVID BELLUSCI

She stared out at noth'n, look'n way
across the river Jesse follows. But black
is creep'n steal'n front and back.
She wrings her sweaty hands
and thinks to read her Holy Book,
but mamma's mind feels confused,
can't think about saint James or John.
She rocks again. Her eyes move
from the plate to Jesse's rifle she
had shot. And climbs a broken chair.
She holds the rifle, but trembl'n just a bit.
And sits, rock'n Jesse's rifle on her lap.
She keeps her eyes wide open.

ONTOLOGY OF BLUE

6 a.m.

        lights or torches
        tudor brick homes
        green firs border streets
        mist creeps through
        Me.
        You?
        sometimes far.
        sometimes near.
        see-through sheers
        enclose the sky
        rain pelts my head
        pipes draining
        roof encases me
        black wings' dirge
        I am not alone.

DAVID BELLUSCI

Dusk

White saucer in the sky
days-old coffee stains, smudged,
nobody to hold the porcelain
left suspended,
cup chipped, black-line crack.

Neither starry nothingness,
    and closed eyelids,
nor nothingness pierced,
    and heavy breath,
smell the dripping brew, softly loud.

The disk floats, withdraws,
silver whispers into a dream,
silk dress robes her
and she vanishes.

Steamy vapours aimlessly rise.

The trucker speeds past, wet roar,
flashing yellow lights, bright signals
races the empty road:
    how's my driving?
    on the fender.
Contact number for comments.

A red saucer placed on the
earth's edge – robust,

pours its scent onto the ground.

Papa put in the firewood.

ONTOLOGY OF BLUE

Third Monday in March

Angel hair skims that orange ball
bidding robins final *farewell*,
whispers lick west into shape.

Ice sheets float south, axed
blocks lost and lose manoeuvring
wild Saint Lawrence deadly pushes
black ribbons.

My boots a metal box hardened
hammered iron my feet numb
a distant shore, king's ships.

Convent drapes drawn, white
candles blown, how early they sleep,
and pray? Five centuries of school
children in starched veil learning.

An orange speck peeks to the east,
rounding stuck to the black strings,
I reach to taste – my feet won't move.

Spring

A green bud pierces the twig
my eyes fixed to a branch.

The village bells toll, the steeple
crisscrossed.

Rococo blue, avian melodies
return, reclaim their turf

bought flowers, yellow,
hide tired grounds.

A baby cries, approaching
in a blue buggy, the father marches
like a guard, protects his baby,
stops, to adjust
the bottle, takes a daffodil, tickles
the little one quiet.

Branches brush bushes,
the father tightly holds
the buggy handle,
looks:
straight ahead, strong hands firm.

The smell of moss,
cobble stones, flower hedges.

A lady in a pink dress gives me
her umbrella.

ONTOLOGY OF BLUE

Buttery grapes*

>*Filthy dirty work,* purple grapes
> quietly polish the glass, coating
> me with oak and jam.
> Forty-six degrees in downtown
> Lodi, arches point to the Golden
> Bear, nuggets and raisins, tasting
> milk and honey. Legends
> of Prohibition, growing pressing
> fermenting at home,
> undisturbed by useless
> money-making codes.
> True blessings in September,
> scent of blackberry,
> old barrels French and Italian,
> now Virginia and Missouri,
> after-taste. Shaking every ninety days.
> Good dirt for olives Mediterranean sun,
> vines dance like David, to excited
> lovers married, and crying babies.
> Baskets of gnarls, women carry
> singing at dawn heaping nature's
> fruit. European names refined,
> pour-taste-test, cool inside.
>
> The bride's mother smells me.

*Lodi, California, U.S.A.

Time

When the black sky opens
greyness unveils forms.
Ripples.
Branches held by trunks.
Geese paddle together.
Drops of water and snow crystals melt.
Ripples.
Cottages speck a distant shore.

SECTION 3

Mango season

ONTOLOGY OF BLUE

Cali

Dreamy substance echoes

lucrative gold pounds slaves across
the ocean – cocoa leaves wait

salsa caleña beats the avenidas,
stands sell *menudos* at 200.

Buses fume, trucks cut you off, cars
revving at red lights

beggars hold cups – plates
boasting veiny hands

standing on one leg, unfolding scars
war decorations.

Our Lady of Mercy flickers candles
devotees in hope – in syllables.

Three crosses on a hill, the Redeemer
arms outstretched, a blessing.

White marble, Andalusian arches
priests in hidden rituals.

Palm trees still listen.

DAVID BELLUSCI

After-school downpour

A boy in uniform stares, holding
his sister's hand, waiting for their parents
or chauffeur to pick them up,
and bring them home, where I know
Maria or Carmela, or Teresa
waits, with a towel and dry clothes,
warm milk and cake.

His back-pack firmly attached,
a turquoise blue, elementary
school logo, *Deus amor est*.
Wet black hair, short and parted,
he runs into the bank shelter
staring at me, and out, rain patters
on glass, eyes on traffic, noisy cars,
blurry stream of lights.

For a minute, a taxi tempts me,
but I follow the old
Colombian with a cane,
drenched, climbing up the hill.

The schoolboy sitting in the back seat
waves from the Mercedes.

ONTOLOGY OF BLUE

Only in Bogota

Rumba in the sun, voices loud,
bodies pulsate,
moonrise unnoticed.

Regaton, Vallenato, Salsa
steps-to-hips, arms swing, backs curve,
little-here, more-there,
¡e-yah! ¡Bueno!
Beer flows, rum, rum, rum
shooters breeze like a gold mill.

Nobody heeds *no-smoking sign*,
puffs and drags,
cigarettes hang low ¡Aviso!

Tables of 3, then 7, now 10.
Bogota is party.

Arms outstretched,
hugging strangers,
lips to ears, someone whispers,
laughter breaks, contagious screams.

Security frisks the body,
feeling what might be.
Tight bodies block the toilets,
walls and floors vibrate with drums.
I wash my hands. He asks me
if I need a towel.

DAVID BELLUSCI

The woman at the table
swings her head –
the weight is too much,
she drops, face down, swings again,
shouting so someone just might hear.

ONTOLOGY OF BLUE

Free coffee

Bogota rains, colombian brews
espresso pumps the machine
exciting my nostrils. Wet shoes, damp pants,

rain pounds the *avenidas*...

cappuccino froth sweet.

The lollipop man standing on a corner
returns to his plastic bag tent,
wondering if he earned a living
in his blue NY baseball cap
counting the lollies.

Holding her baby, walking with her man,
image of mamma, tired worn wrinkle faced.

The carriage jerks to the rhythm
of horses, squeezed by yellow taxis,
smoke-glassed buses.
They stop at the red light,
the horses ignore the flashes
and the driver's whips.
A boy sits with papa or *tio* startled
by the racing traffic.
Only the pots and trinkets
utter syllables.

Fountains outside sprinkling,
café bar hisses a European feel,
stainless Italian marble, azaleas hang
venetian pastries. The shop has a promotion,
free coffee with breakfast.*

She doesn't even understand my Spanish,
I wanted cream in my coffee –
and dessert ...

---

* *Gratis todo el café por lo comprar de nuestros desayunos* – Free coffee with the purchase of our breakfasts.

ONTOLOGY OF BLUE

Broken bed

Campodos* a place
for the punished,
atomic sun, Colombian guerrillas,
freedom for cocaine.
Victor's hardened nurse knuckles,
beer buddy un-uniformed.
Entra!
Scratchy voice, squeaky, calls,
frame falling, cracked walls,
webs coating corners, I force
a sweaty door.
He lies in his bed,
shredding sheet covers, bare
legs awfully exposed, wrinkled flesh
layered.
Somebody's grandfather, husband,
borrowed suit, useless ring, that wedding.
Grizzle faced, grey, greasy
head, flattened hair-to-the-side,
he calls me, arms outstretched.
"¡Hola!"
Who fed this soul each day?
Villagers?
Bony fingers reach me, fingers
join mine, his, afraid I might
hurt him.

¿Cómo está?
A chair to my left, bamboo pieces.
I sit, his eyes glued to my face.
Furniture to my right,
a toilet.
Gracias, he says.
My hands empty.
"De nada."

---

*Town on the Colombian-Venezuelan border.

ONTOLOGY OF BLUE

Santa Marta

Spanish clouds cover the waves
boys whistle, the cry of babes

floating on water, mothers laugh
bright bikini girls tanned boys splash

orange and green tight dresses,
stalked by men in glasses

underwear at the hips just to tease
rolling vendors of candy and beer

grilled meat, body message cheap
a chair and jars of creams

while boats skim Caribbean foam
rock the waves, touch the shore

sun disappears, sand decorates in pink
shapes of blown animals, orange green

he plays soccer with his dog,
refusing to let go holds the ball

vallenato sounds & rhythms heard
strings at sunset and accordion

bar is carted along the beach
regaton blasts, music and muscles

sell the stuff, bear-chested men wear
rosaries around their neck

woman covered in the sand
detailed breasts in a mould to match

aguardiente goes around
mother to daughter, father to son

vendors chant their rum,
late-night Medellin 'til 4 a.m.

ONTOLOGY OF BLUE

Installing the President

Flags, base half yellow,
red blue horizontals,
dot houses, color rooftops.
Machine guns line *La Settima*
soldiers, police security,
supermercados and intersections,
patrol ...
bangs into sunset regaton.

Abierto for coffee, Sunday morning
hangovers observe the Sabbath.
Plastic shoes, bags and cells on display,
streets washed and swept.
City silence extinguishes each fire.
I spot a man sit, too early to beg,
he scares me, the size of his head,
bloody eyes, thousands of wrinkles.
He holds a plastic cup,
elephant sickness or leprosy,
flesh battles the soul.

Bogota's guilt hides in the lush
plantations, in velvet theatre seats,
chain-link fences, rifled guards,
Doberman attacks.

A beggar or drunkard hit by a car,
nobody touches him.

DAVID BELLUSCI

Bombin hat*

>Her hand on her wrinkled face,
>hiding from me.
>Eyes pushing away foul words
>black hair under a bombin
>like English bowler hats.
>I smell her sweat.
>
>High, her forehead raised
>shaking away soldiers,
>crooked lines cutting her skin.
>Chewing open syllables
>of mourning. Ripped lips.
>Her spaced teeth. I hear
>her chew tobacco.
>
>Nine children around mamma,
>little hands reaching tightly.
>
>I pushed my thoughts out
>and took mamma into my arms.
>They shot papa, I know,
>fingers pointed, fists fought,
>they shot papa dead.
>
>Mamma's eyes stare into mine,
>kids turn around, waiting …
>String of images before me,
>
>I fold the newspaper.

* Bowler hat worn by women in Bolivia and Peru.

ONTOLOGY OF BLUE

Doña Marcela

Airport parking only a dollar,
she speeds in her silver Lexus,
announces our arrival on her cell.
Graffiti slums, beggars on guard.
Sausages fry, corn smokes.
Her blood red nails point
to Christmas trees *all year round,*
Doña's politics skid the circle,
her voice shrieks,
a *bruja* thinks her husband's Christ,
magic spell for votes.
Seism-sensitive Cathedral,
stands fragile, as if waiting for doomsday.
A pure-blood Nica, kerchief unfolds,
suggests a coffee or menu.
Doña her tone deeper,
prolongs syllables, *espresso, por favor.*
When John-Paul visited, Ortega's mob,
Mass interrupted, his holy sigh,
si-len-ci-o.
Strolling with Viola, hands joined,
President and Pope, She and He.
Tin cans, plastic bags attached to walls,
guarded fortress, cloistered nuns,
eleven shades, from white to black,
Mexican and Salvadorian.
Iron soldiers, rifles in the air,

a round-about reminder,
or signs of hope,
each driver, trucker, scooter, onlooker.
No appointment for university rector
– or whoever is in charge on a Saturday
morning – security keeps the window open
for *Doña*. Phone rings, lets her pass,
she strides, *I told you …*
And *Masaya volcano closed to visitors,*
the *Doña* insists, her third attempt,
just a quick peek at crater and smoke.
Gates open. Volcanic helmets on.
In town, Regeton blasts in the parking lot,
the pick-up next to *Doña*, a child
in the driver's lap, *No, that's peligroso,*
and then shops, chateau wine.
Ace jumps to the car window,
runs after his *Doña*, the car manoeuvred
like a plane onto a runway, barricaded
in cement slabs, a solid wall laced
with charred glass and electric wires,
enclosing palms, papaya,
oak tables and iron bells.
A housekeeper serving for thirty years
sets breakfast in the patio, pineapple,
mild coffee, rice, beans, an egg
– *guaya pinto* – with toasted bread.

ONTOLOGY OF BLUE

> *Doña* tells her watchman to find bullets,
> an unloaded rifle, useless.
> When darkness hangs, birds caw,
> the night-time drizzle comforts and threatens.
> *Doña* brakes, hoots her horn, the guard
> next door appears. Her rosary stops.
> *Hola, I need bullets,*
> *and show Rodrigo how to use it.*
> *I'm on my way to Church.*
> Beads slip through her smooth fingers.
>
> The nuns know her sister.
>
> Six shots fired,
> light rain only at night.

Managua, Nicaragua, August, 2012

Luna azúl*

Trident shot violently
north of the equator, ripping the
falling curtains. Hidden skies,
craters in the clouds.
Neptune belts naked palms
hit by ruthless pellets.
Whips. Atlantic a massive
stretch of vengeance.
Lashing at me.
Thrashes of hate.
Flashes of war. Untriggered
rage.
Silver shots sprayed
across the shore. Silence.
A shield of light beams
into my shaken room. Silence.
Ripples of blue brush the ocean.
I withdraw. Silence.
Silver foil path meanders
beyond the quiet splashes
and blue moon.

* *Pacific coast of Central America*

Oaxáca's grasshoppers

Potholes, danger signs missing,
I hug the dusty Ford.
His fingers, *por allí ... por allá ...*
the peppery smells of fried chorizo
overpower his index and Oaxáca's
syllables.
Mexicana bankrupt, explains
cracked cement structures,
chipped paint, *aquí estoy,* humming
Ana Gabriel.
Chapulines, he shouts. I dare not,
pequeño golden ones or pimento-red
muy grande.
I swallow Tequila and stilettos
in the square. Ranchero colonnades,
black lamps light Juarez arches,
hidden revolutionaries.
Mariachis never far playing
for blonde gringos.
She sits in her corner,
hand stretched, *señor, por favor.*
Pathetic sight, the two
her baby covered in a dirty pink
blanket. Her cup empty.
I turn around and walk
back to the smelly spot.

DAVID BELLUSCI

Man in the pick-up

It rains dirt.
A filthy white pick-up inches
into a remote village.
Locals stare,
mothers embrace
babies tight; fathers
take their little boys' hands.
A stiff assembly
of rainy-season bodies.
The cattle kraal fence,
marks the boundary.
Half-naked children
stare. And stare.
Noses runny, licking mucus
flies stick.
A mamma points,
an extended finger. A baby
cries and cries.
Unwashed heads, the head
disease.
A white man sits in the pick-up,
behind a window,
barely open …
he can be seen:
strange smile,
pig-like skin,
dried-apple lips,
scaring the babies.

ONTOLOGY OF BLUE

Tea in secret
   (or, Thoughts of Doris Lessing)

      Past treaties, chiselled horses,
bronze busts – Nonsense!
Playing with the ballots, people say,
leaflets and tracts and ads,
educating voters.
Freedom Struggle, fought,
screaming blood, hunted women,
(accused witches), Rhodesian
sell-outs, local traitors:
      all guilty.
Debits settled, farmers re-settled.
Justice the chiefs cry, the axe
for revenge.
Lessing knew the farms.
A newspaper story opens
her 1950 novel:
      servant accused of a crime
      taboo love affair in a home
      woman murdered
          a house-keeper!
          her lover?
          who knows…
Nature follows its own course:
      vicious criminal,
      compassionate healer,
      stealer of sorts.
He only served her tea.

DAVID BELLUSCI

Beauty's Restaurant

Saturday shopping before markets close
at 1 p.m. One-day getaway
from a forgotten mission, teachers, ex-pats
flirt here with check-out counters and electricity.
Rhodesia's colonial Fort Victoria,
a refaced Masvingo.

A sweaty woman lisps, repeats my order,
she seems huge. English syllables, some
Bantu (South African linguists say that's
pejorative), her thick fingers,
raised eyebrows advertise her specials.

Simbarashe* smells of sweat, solidly sits
claiming our table in Beauty's crowded
eatery. Vinyl blue tops match plastic
blue chairs. Flies buzz over spilled rice.

Beauty's Restaurant, mamma's dream,
free Coke glasses with beef orders.
No beer, but Fanta is drunk, local favourite
green cream soda, you know, pink at home.

She serves pounds of mealie, or *sadza*
in this language, or rice if you want to pay more.
Simbarashe ignores the cold silver cutlery, his
fingers in the relish, red tomatoes and onions.

* *Zimbabwean (Shona) male name, "power of God."*

Thomas Mapfumo, the Bundu Boys ...
marimba keys, leather bongos, the music
like *peri peri,* sweaty.

It will be dark when we return
the mission withdrawn, strange forest.

Hyenas will smell meat on our breath.
They always have.

DAVID BELLUSCI

Guerrillas

    Smudge marks disturb the glass
stripes alter Laurier street.
Man in a corner table wears his
politics. Known names, Kinshasa –
Goma – Kigali ... Congolese
war, Great Lakes fragmented.

♦♦♦♦

I stood secretly watching soldiers
march, dark green uniforms,
berets, virile voices, sweaty faces,
emptying streets.
Lingala chants.
Smell of balcony mould.
Room overlooking Lake Khivu
like 1950 posters,
Sabena Belgian ads with colonial visits.
Rounding architecture shape oval
balconies, a reminder of lost land,
rebels' victory.

Shores bordered by green,
    one-time markets
    coffee plantations
    guerrilla game parks
    before the war.

Locals recognised me
as a white stranger in Lubumbashi.

ONTOLOGY OF BLUE

Or Elizabethville.

Not far away below the hills,
where the mist settles,
I avoided the silverback's eyes.

DAVID BELLUSCI

Nigerian dream

His cowhide jacket rugged fit,
shoulder lapels mark his frame.
The maroon scarf, Italian
silk-satin mix, drapes over his neck,
falls smooth on his side.

Dark chocolate corduroy pants,
slim cut, trace his legs,
black leather shoes.

I wondered about the scar on his forehead,
angel stitches healed black on black.

*My mom says hello, she's back home
now.*

We met because of his mother's dream:
worried
praying
true friend for her son,
tucked away at university.
Methane, sex and all-night parties not for her boy.

He sticks out his hand, a bag. *Here, for you,
from where I work. I hope it fits.*

Big smiles appear natural
with some people.

ONTOLOGY OF BLUE

Visit*

>His bike helmet hanging, clenched,
>"Shall I wait for you, sir?"
>The torch burned in the African
>heat. His eyes counting coins,
>palm opened.
>
>"It's alright," I looked
>at his eyes set on mine.
>
>A quiet smile ... backing up.
>
>The wind brightened the flames,
>a sound of banners shouting words,
>pointing fingers at visitors not knowing
>past stories, painting street stones,
>dusty paths, shallow streams, deep red.
>
>Guarded doors, cheaply made,
>hiding secrets on display.
>
>Corridors, unlit, streams of words,
>to be read, more in-form-ation.
>A woman cries, a man stares,
>at reconfigured bodies,
>smouldering huts,
>torched churches.
>
>The man cries.
>
>My tribe, your tribe, their tribe.
>Who really cares!
>The tribe of humans.

Our skeletons.

Voices, strange sounds I hear,
words choked in shock.
The woman holds her head, shaking.

Child's sneakers, muddy white,
laceless, maybe 4 or 5 years old.
"NY" stitched on a baseball cap.
Dark red smudged on blue.
Green orange prints on a sarong,
soiled, mud-stained, dragged.
A cracked cane, broken glasses,
t-shirt flying "We are the world."
Faces on paper, stringed, pinned,
neat rows, life hanging smiles,
school uniforms, skin shining,
clay water jugs, thatched baskets.

Skulls in rows, yellowish white,
staring at empty hands, useless
words, waiting.

Split skulls, mark of the axe.
Skulls with small holes, bullet shot.
Small skulls, cracked.

Clubs below to end that scream,
to punish friends, relatives ...

Outside he waited, hand tight,
helmet in his hand, *allons* ...

* *National Memorial of Rwanda*

ONTOLOGY OF BLUE

Listen!

>You can't feel my pain, you don't:
>– shiny screen –
>know my worries, you don't care
>about the blood spilled
>– more Wiki info –,
>Why should you?
>*A Pontic-Greek on Facebook who*
>*pleads his case, genocide: enough!*
>– Pontus, where's that? –
>*His Turkish town a target.*
>– as in Turkish delight, they're jelly red.
>And you have the Hurons on your mind,
>nothing to do with India.
>– I know First Nations –
>Iroquois trade, the drums, the beats.
>–Yes, the music! –
>You're still thinking about the
>Cruise, Caribbean again, or perhaps
>like the shirts you wear, Hawaii.
>– Well, yeees –
>Believing your son unjustly treated,
>in jail, when he should be in rehab.
>– It cost my yacht –
>And your body aching, last night's
>romance, won't leave you, or him, or her …
>– It won't last long –

Threats carried out in the 1900s,
since the 1500s.
– Inquisition or Reformation –
I know of much worse,
when God said,
from paradise
       you will be banished ...

ONTOLOGY OF BLUE

Monsoon petals*

Mud drives our Land Cruiser
orange red saris disappear,
black plastic raincoats thrown over.
Squeaky wipers splash, a dirty
rag to clear the foggy glass,
monsoon rains blast coconut trees,
road repossessed.
The old man ignores us,
our noisy engine, pedals as if the mud
belongs to him, his head looks straight,
his hands sturdy, his legs in rhythmic
circular motion.
Dirty columns of still-standing mansions
with Portuguese names. Who lives in them?
Blue Marian shrines, incense smoke dying,
decorated in *phool mala*, necklaces of yellow
devotion.
He carefully parks his rusty bike
where the Hindu temple waits.
We speed past throwing up mud.
I am greeted
with folded hands centred at his lips,
small-beaded Rosary hangs,
a nod. I bow my head:
our eyes meet.

Goa, India, July, 2013

DAVID BELLUSCI

Coconut chutney

Coconut chutney in lotus hands,
a metal bowl covered in soft texture
offered to me. I scoop my breakfast,
tongue waits like a dog for that
teasing meat, the scent hidden
that buds detect.
I lick. The creamy coconut paste
dissolves, my tongue
curls and stretches, the white
groundnut succumbs to green chili leaving
sharp barb-wired taste
to trigger lateral clicks.
Green chili burns me up. Whiff
of exotic seed encased,
protects a hard unwilling shell
and sweet. I allow coriander to coat,
my mouth tasting powder.
I dream my tongue rubs into a chili:
I lick. I chew. I swallow
the coconut chutney.

Double-burger avenue

    Sky hides an icy glare.
    Naked trees stand exposed.
    Winter exhausts tire-worn snow
    finished in shoe prints
    and coke-stains.
    Mud-splattered cars mechanically
    stop at the blinking red box,
    an audience.
        Laser Hair Removal ... Stay Slim
        Fitness,
    mock me sitting at a window table,
    mouth full of fries.
    A fat pedestrian in tight green
    jacket looks in and slips,
    rescuing himself like an acrobat
    on the same spot speaking to his mic.
    Hammered in Victorian bricks
    French sign reads *égalité* in a marble
    plaque. First Nations and Acadians
    waiting. Bloody revolutions of choking
    ideology and machete tyranny they
    name *liberté*. Allegiance to the
    Gutenberg machinery.

    Living in a cave –

Christmas in Chicago

      Chili peppers & jalapeños,
      ground meat,
           tomatoes thick,
I sit. I stir.
American Gold hits
Me,

big-mouths, they announce,
now departing
        green strings,
        yellow lights
        blinking blue
        – tracing walls.

Flames, *con carne* kitchen.

Where's Kevin,

      … I look around …
For the mom to sell her soul,
      at the Xmas counter,
for a flight?
to Detroit?

Martinis, ciders, and glogg,
mulled wine … egg nog,
spicy candy cane coffee.

– clouds drop – on target –

Sagittarius holds my arch!

ONTOLOGY OF BLUE

American connections

Sea-Tac airport thrilled me, Tacobel counters,
TexMex my first time. But no wings to fly on.

We parked for a GQ visit, photos of *moi:*
Dutch jacket, Givenchy scarf, Italian black gloves.

My flight overbooked, Boston replaced Toronto,
rerouted on SwissAir out of Rome –
and Zurich.

Lansing airport – a conference – Michigan State
in Autumn prep world of binders and jeans
and bespeckled speakers.

Detroit's airport and a NorthWest journey,
no time for MacDo.

I flied through Dallas, *visiting Laredo
of all places. Does that count?* Desert retreat.

US Airways from Tel Aviv: I like
to say I had Golden Star,
then, coffee and sticky buns in Philly.

Stop at Denver, discovered *Max and Erma's*:
Kentucky ale, tortilla soup. They ask for I.D. here.
Chequered apron server taps, *It's the law.*

Cincinnati on Delta –
t-shirt read, *Ohio State,* then, I knew ...

Mexicana bankrupt rescued rescheduled:
Phoenix.

Managua to Houston US border official deadly:
    – *alcohol* WITH *you?*
    – *no,* ON *the plane.*
    – *I'll ask one last time …!*
Immigration disagreed with my preposition.

Disconnected Sacramento, *how can
you do this to me?*
But I can talk about California wine!
Bombay to Newark non-stop United, polished
announcements weather-route-service,
and fifteen hours of Bollywood.

I still refuse the body scanner.

ONTOLOGY OF BLUE

Arrivals

      Connecting flights, Heathrow industrial
      blown
      cologne counters, driving scents
      erotic Givenchy, Dolce Gabbana,
      she sprays me her Davidoff promo.
      Saxon blonde hair
      drapes
      slender shoulders,
      satin shawl,
      her turquoise eyes fixed on me,
      her bottle tilted
      – my wrist, unnoticed. Marked.
      She whispers numbers, soaks
      my skin,
      her specialty. I submit, passively.
      My plane flexing at the gate, ready
      to soar.
      Our two minutes of mist
      spellbound:
      she changes my destiny:
      Scheduled to Delayed.

Airport shuttle

She wears shoes dripping a puddle – blue umbrella, a rusty metal tip – young man, a high-school dropout returns from the airport – a young woman stands, falling asleep, moss green stockings with runs and holes, tight trendy – black boots, purple top hangs loose hidden under a leather jacket – the crying won't stop, the lady hasn't fed her baby, nobody sees her, only the baby in the buggy – I wonder if the father sits with them – moist windows, we see nothing, hear the cars, the buses, the trucks – heavy loud rains splash on windows – breathing moistens the glass – a covered woman in her *hijab* makes a statement, I guess we all do – the man wears his wide-rimmed black hat and narrates history like Abraham – *Visit New Zealand – Backpackers Africa – Shrines of Italy* – I'm on a domestic flight … then what? – The two Asian women sound Japanese, sweet, and high-pitched – another stop … where's the airport? – I wonder what the Arabs are saying? – I give up, German sounds the same – How could he read a paper? probably a student, master of motion blonde and diligent – she has gone through her text messages fifty times by now – so, has everyone else – or listening to the pod: ears plugged, selected sounds wired – I wonder if they see me?

SECTION 4

Mosaics Made in Italy

ONTOLOGY OF BLUE

Summer breeze in southern Italy

White sheets uncovered bed,
curtains blown by wind.
Revving Vespa shifts speeds,
buses, brakes screech, another bike.
Saucers piled cups and spoons rinsed
restaurant dishwashing clatter.
Bells toll 9 p.m., a basilica for Mary.

◆◆◆◆

On the balcony, stretched on a patio
chair I hear mamma talking to her cousin,
the dialect she reserves for her brother at home.
She laughs, Concetta laughs.
I look up at the sky, dark blue
new world, old world
my eyes close hearing
mamma's voice.

Early-evening breeze, cooler night
darker, my shoes feel light.
Quietly, I wake up not knowing the fizzy water
my *zia* brings me, I thought 7-Up,
tasting tasteless they call *San Pellegrino*.

◆◆◆◆

The bell tower in front, row of statues
of Renaissance Popes, popular saints,
people hurrying through bronze doors.

I enter and say a prayer for mamma.

Mamma's home

Immigrated or dead, two hundred remain
embodied behind brick walls,
behind the cobble-stone streets. When Mary
appears in May greeting villagers one
arm raised the other holding her crowned
Son, *paesani** bodies increase.
Each May She processes in the village
solemn fanfare raising up Her Son.

*Zii** and *cuginetti** appear from Rome,
Frankfurt, Chicago,
bring gifts filled with nostalgia.

Mamma's cousin hugged me, calling
out my name, my first visit at twelve.
Zia cooked *penne* & *verdura**. Their
house overlooked the greenest valley.
Now shiny Renaults and Audis fill small
spaces, squeezing through narrow
roads under arches built for horses.

Faces unknown. August exchanges.

*paesani** – *neighbours from the same village*
*Zii** – *aunts and uncles*
*cuginetti** – *little cousins*
*verdura** – *penne and spinach*

ONTOLOGY OF BLUE

*Vecchiarelle** sit and stare, in black
dresses, tempted to ask about my family.
Within sacred Romanesque
walls I hear, *Si, si, I know her,
you have her eyes; we baked bread
together; we met al forno*;
we stitched lace for the Madonna.*
Last Summer a woman in her black
shawl stood outside the Church doors.
*Mammate** lived next to my house.
She moved briskly on the wet steps.
*Questè la casa di mamma**.

The gentle villager, a living relic, invites me
to taste the sticky sweet homemade lemon
liqueur, *limoncello*.

A picture hangs on her kitchen wall,
handsome man with deep dark eyes
and smooth dark brows, a trimmed beard.
Her voice pierces the quiet: "*frattame**,
he was in love with your mother."

*Vecchiarelle** – little old ladies*
*al forno** – oven*
*Mammate** – your mother*
*Questè la casa di mamma** – this is your mother's house*
*frattame** – my brother*

DAVID BELLUSCI

Stranger in a village

Smell of horses in the house,
purring cats possess a kitchen,
flies stick to spoons and goat cheese.
Papa a stranger in his village,
to the closest city he flees,
sits at a hotel dinner table, covered
in white linen, service in silver cutlery
bottles of his favourite, *Chianti*,
and *aqua minerale frizzante**, orders *cappellini
con pomodoro**, and *vitello al limone*.;*

Confused about his brother,
      – How could he expect us to eat?
drain outside, cats all over, ashes in the fire place.
      – Papa, that's where he lives.

❖❖❖❖

The odours remain but not as pungent
when I return years later without papa,
notice their resemblance eyes and cheeks
I visit the War Memorial: *Dispersi in Guerra**.
Mussolini sent soldiers to freeze
disastrous campaign, the Russian front
nonna's son never returned, only nineteen.

aqua minerale frizzante* – carbonated mineral water
capppellini con pomodoro* – capppellini with tomato
vitello al limone* – veal with lemon
Dispersi in Guerra* – Missing in War

My cousin cooks *i troccatelle**,
while *zio's** cats clear the mice like a vacuum,
flies still annoy, but the horse smell
has almost disappeared.
The *capretto** cheese they make is salty,
I think – delicious.

In *America* they die
without talking to each other.

*i troccatelle** – *dialect (Foggia): type of linguini pasta*
*zio's** – *uncle's*
*capretto** – *goat*

DAVID BELLUSCI

Halifax 1955

Shuffling on the deck and bridge, process
of immigration customs Canadian control
officers in polished uniforms check arrivals
form "with/out papers":
health documents and belongings
forbidden Genova salami, confiscate
a precious Saint Anthony.

English and French unknown languages,
Sisters in blue habits translate.

Sick from the voyage, merciless January
waves, you are confused about questions
uttered in strange consonants.

Proud in your suit, respectful dress, dignified,
you wear elegant fabrics, charcoal
blue and grey, Italian leather shoes.

The journey not over, you bid *farewell,
God keep you.*

Train stationed on tracks waits to take you
West across the endless white desert.

Frontier post. Sawmill town.

Tucked in your bag,
a copy of the Homeland.*

---

* Greek-registered ship used by Italian immigrants in the 1950s.

Afternoon tuna

A clay jar filled with bouncing olives
shiny black skins oil dripping. Next,
I imagine the taste of pinky-white tuna
flipping chunks in front of me.
I signal signora Gerardi who speaks
to me in Italian. I notice her beauty
mark, it's fake.
She prepares my panino at the counter.
I point and she slices the soft bread
stuffing it with tomatoes, tuna,
mozzarella and olives.
She adds basil. It's Friday.
Mamma waits at the back of her
newly opened children's wear shop, sitting
beside the grey filing cabinet. She
holds her coffee in one hand, muffin
in the other.
The noisy winter heater is on, the smell
of hot wires a reminder.

I sit close to mamma on a little footstool
and tell her about Sister Margret
and detention. The phone rings.
Sister wears a white veil
covering her hair and forehead. But her
blue eyes, severe that day: I angered
Sister insulting a pupil. Mamma cried.
I never forgot Sister for upsetting
mamma and our lunch together.

ONTOLOGY OF BLUE

Blue harbour

In a photo you wear a yellow knit sweater
finger points to *nonna's* gift from Italy
blue eyes focused on your little brothers.

When I studied Dante you visited me
stayed in my university res that summer
accompanied me home on the ferry.

Don't worry be happy, that song you liked.
Reminiscing at Schwartz Bay, I thought
of you. You can still make me cry.

I dreamed about you chasing after a ball
sweating, a determined player making
the league in Italy, professional soccer.

Now you bring me to Italian bistros,
English pubs and ritzy hotels.
Remembering Friday, fish you order.

You think of white sangria. We drink
to music of boats docking
after Mass, a sun-filled morning,

You are the six-year old in my novel
holding my hand with your questions,
and the teenager of my first poem.

Your inquisitive tone replays Toronto
and Calgary, prayers we shared in Assisi,
Lourdes, *gelati* in Madrid and Rome.

Your peach ties, blue shirts, cashmere
jackets match for the office, black gym
sweats for workouts on the track field.

Table decorated with *gnocchi,* bottles of wine
you're focussed on mamma teasing papa,
now we talk women, finding you a wife …

Cappuccini

> Nutella cornetto,
> folded in a serviette, I ordered
> before my cappuccino. First client
> in Rome, a Saturday morning.
> He asks if I'll have this *qui**.
> *Certo**, I think, point
> to a waiting table in polite Italian.
> We'll bring you the cappuccino.
> I sit facing the piazza, hearing
> piping sounds of espresso steam.
> Creamy chocolate hazelnut
> coats my tongue, the coffee ritual
> begins: waiter arrives smoothly
> places the cappuccino in front of me
> the *Lavazza* label green and white.
> Rituals of Rome, market tents
> rise like huge porcini mushrooms,
> *grappa* cheaper than statues of Mary.
> Red-gold flaps, flags hail Nero
> or Caligula or some other god.
> I scratch my ankle,
> *were his feet as big as mine?*

*qui** – *here*
*Certo** – *certainly*

DAVID BELLUSCI

◆◆◆◆

My nephew prefers the other
Italian bistro opposite
the Chinese market.
He likes the washrooms.
On Commercial drive, once-upon
-a-time-centre for *Italo-Vancouveresi*,
he brings me to Italian coffee
specialty, orders two cappuccini.
The Italian ambience heavy,
exaggerated tricolours –
green-white-red coat the bar
like cheap paint, marble tables fake
Made in Italy. Silver chairs,
black seat covers – leather perhaps.
David stands, full body, white details,
Julius Caesar, his lined face,
Roman high society. Brick walls,
frescoed ceiling, black and white
celebrity photos – Dean Martin,
Frank Sinatra, Gina Lollobrigida,
Sofia Loren. A church bell, a sacred
touch. Soldier, for Hadrian's army?
Medieval Knight, defending Siena.
Cement fountain for coins like Trevi.

Tiramisù

Garlic and onion sizzle in olive oil
hot pan, medium flame, ground beef,
peppered, crushed tomatoes, basil,
simmer, made for *rigatoni* and *romano*.

White linen table, Murano goblets
purple red, crystal colours, rising neck
flower bouquets, redden soft lips
endless Tuscan gardens, grapes ready.

Pressing gently, sweet taste
love-potion, head dizzy wild *Strega**

injects my heart my blood my brains
confusing me: bewitched enchanted.

Buongiorno: fasten your seatbelts.
Ferrari-like engines blast clouds
Risotto & *gelato* 10-hour Gravol,
cruising altitude, more *Dolce Vita*.

Magazine cover, Botticelli's *Venere*
standing in her shell, Firenze her home.
Frangelico's cosmic feathers shades
of geen, wings melt into Italian gold.

Strega* – "*Witch*" – *name of liqueur.*

Sicilian cannoli

Happy Mother's Day on his cell,
she waits all Sunday searching
for his smile, weekly visits as if her son.

He failed to drop by, not even a call,
he really did try.

The woman's husband explains,
they once had a son, his age now.

Evenings together, espresso, Sicilian
pastries and stories. Orders of cannoli
for a bank charity, a neighbourhood
fund-raiser.

He drives to see her the next Sunday,
at the hospital she waits. Memories
of his own grandmother. Summer
emergencies, weekly. That endless
August.

Say a prayer for her.
Adopted. Loved. He feels the duty.
Dinner discussions, her level of cancer.

But levels destroy hope
more than cells.

ONTOLOGY OF BLUE

Lost in the city

Name of a French saint, vision of Mary.
Your eyes blue, skin fair soft
like your mother's, dressed in satin,
floral Italian prints for Thanksgiving.

Nonna taught you to make homemade
lasagna, your little fingers holding each
layer. Your Saturday treat. Or chore?

Your school uniform, navy-blue
like your brothers'. Mamma's little girl,
one day a teacher, a dream.

You look in the mirror feeling your need
to lose weight. Who said? Your jeans feel
tight, mamma's cooking, you say, the button
won't close on your black shirt.

Large gold earrings, gift bought in Florence.
Black mascara lines your eyelashes,
drying artfully your bleach-blonde hair.

Your tongue when you laugh sparkles,
pierced by a stud ring. You think
I never noticed.

Nobody knows, except some friends
selling French perfume,

why you left home.

DAVID BELLUSCI

Feeling guilty

Zio Rafaele persisted,
I waited for you until 2 in the morning.

My tired pictures, words,
Who asked you to wait? You gave me the key.

His eyes wide, eyebrows thick grey,
and repeated, *I waited and waited.*
You never showed up.

Zia Giovanna stood in the kitchen,
thick glasses magnified her eyes,
a green wool skirt in July
hands on her hips, *When did you arrive?*

I smiled, *Ciao, zia how are you?*
Yesterday.

Her hands trembled, *And today you come to visit?*

Yes, delayed. A long trip from Canada.
She invites me for lunch, explaining,
First you visit the eldest zia or zio,
not the cousins. They come after.

I apologized, *Scusate*, zia.*

We have a shot of *grappa* in the morning,
and at night we drink homemade wine,
and *Vecchia Romagna*, when necessary.

Scusate* – Excuse me

Jumpity-Jump

Papa pushes the wheel-barrel,
mamma plants the bulbs, nonna's
flowers in a back yard where
zucchini and tomato grow, a goldfish
pond splashes, the Virgin gracefully prays.

He reads about electricity, studies hard,
works with wires, and important stuff,
pages strewn, diagrams symbols
memorised.

Mamma's gonna be a soccer mom,
kicks hard, shoots to win: stand back!

Four weeks before you breathed
she screamed on the plastic slide
a summertime sprinkler
launching
drenched
sliding on her back, legs in the air.

I hear papa yell for the first time,
… *you better not!* … but mamma
howls laughing, papa bends over
as if waiting to deliver you.

DAVID BELLUSCI

On the Labour Day weekend,
Colombia, Mexico, home to kiss you,
I first met you.

So tiny in my arms, fingernails manicured
by God, so quiet, wrapped in an Italian
shawl, a miracle from heaven in pink knits.
Your eyes softly closed
your lips thin, red
your soft breathing ...

I hold you the way your papa slept
in my arms.

My plane waits...

ONTOLOGY OF BLUE

Papa's watch

The gold Bulova papa wore
for Christmas, Easter,
Weddings and Funerals, I chose.

Self-winding.
A purchase in Italy, Milan I think.

Papa the mechanic, in greasy jeans
a filthy cap dirty hands stretched
under a car, on special occasions
put gel in his hair, wore grey-like
Versace, and his gold watch.

Mamma chose his ties
purple-blue diamond.

While I taught at a mission
in Bujumbura
reaching from my mosquito net
papa's watch dropped –

Jeweller displays *watch-repair*
and worked on papa's Bulova,
thousand bucks the charge!

A week later, the hands wiggled
like they needed therapy.
A missing piece the same jeweller
smiled, her father's costly labour,
three hundred dollars more, *please*.

Alas! Gold hands fixed, reassured
I made my exit
with my father's precious gift. Four
days past, time stopped … hands stuck.
I took my receipts and gold Bulova,

I am left timeless.

Relics

The empty space stands out,
nothing covers the off-white shapes.
I stare at the coat-of-arms – I
once traced and ordered.

Rooms transformed overnight:
papa's Italian newspapers
bundled in blue elastic bands –
black and white family photos
and Don Urbano, gone.

The last visit stung me kitchen walls
deformed:
red heart and arms stretched saying,
Mom, I love you this much,
now an outline in yellow
above the birch cabinet.

Mamma left us ten years ago,
we keep her dresses and shoes
in the small corridor closet.

Papa joined mamma five years ago.
I still sit on his round chair
he bought in the fifties.

I hid this relic in my room ...

DAVID BELLUSCI

Fontana di Trevi

    A pharmacy dated fifteen fifty-two
    a piazza with Benetton green,
    lit icon of Mary.
    Gushing fountains, Baroque cascades,
    three falls, Greek triads made Roman
    – only syllables at dawn.
    Ocean his bulging body of muscle
    stands, his eternal shell. Thick hair
    and chiselled abdomen wash in endless
    streams of water.
    Sensuous woman Abundance bears fruit;
    and Health wears her laurel.
    Fabrics fold in heavy vertical layers
    carving breast and snake.
    Half horse half fish earth and ocean
    sacred in created cosmos.
    Papal insignia and crown, three popes,
    two Clements, one Benedict,
    XII - XIII - XIV, natural springs,
    Water to be enjoyed for good health.
    Popes commission transcendent
    matter, *salus,** and fountains.
    Visitors in panama hats,
    board shorts and muscle shirts, click.
    Lovers kiss in selfies.
    Tour bus drowns the fountain,
    my hand in the blue water.

salus* – health, salvation

ONTOLOGY OF BLUE

Silence of the Tiber

>Tiber arches built in early
>twentieth century, a King's dream
>parallel to the pilgrim's bridge,
>Baroque entry Castel Sant'Angelo.
>Here shielded Angels and stoic Romans
>fight side by side.
>Sun breaks through lighting
>Vittorio Emanuele's triumph.
>Waving palms salute Caesar's laurel.
>Waters ripple gently, seagulls soar,
>a goose leads her goslings.
>White posts and open-mouthed lions
>shape the regal bridge.
>Car horns fade the song of sparrows.
>San Giovanni dei Fiorentini imposes
>on one side, borgo Santo Spirito
>the other. Bells toll seven a.m.
>Rome rises to eternal calls. Tiber
>listens. Angels bring
>Caesar to God.
>Ascending marble and iron of St. Peter's
>copula and Cross,
>King on his knees.

DAVID BELLUSCI

Roman torches

        Cobblestones of Via Cavour bake in June,
        Lady of the Snows brings no relief.
        Pizza lovers chew on tomatoes and cheese,
        at candlelit tables chequered table cloths.
        Gelati limone, cioccolato, crema
        melt in the evening *passeggiata**
        towards the Coliseum.
        Ancient stones, Roman columns
        hiding secrets. Screams of ripping flesh,
        roar of spectators. Lamb-like the civil
        misfits are led to the slaughter.
        Threats of perdition call to reject power
        and lust, to love someone hated.
        Their message scorned. Confused zealots,
        demented fanatics, simple followers
        of an esoteric movement from the East.
        Via dei Imperatori processions of Caesars
        leads to the republican piazza
        where the goddess of Rome stands,
        King's protectress.
        Incense rises from the temples and shrines
        of martyrs whose sacred bones
        replace Caesars.

*passeggiata** *– walk*

ONTOLOGY OF BLUE

Capes and hoods*

> Silence, the Venetian lagoon at night
> demands. One-time university
> friendships bonding in the name of
> Plato, Aristotle and God.
> Monastery. City.
> Monk. Politician.
> Patricians all of them.
> Departures. Deaths.
> Cloister smells of hunger,
> procession of black tunics
> in lighted candles, Vespers.
> Sunset on cemetery island.
> I hear requests as I leave the boat,
> the iron doors open.
> The lion's fame envelopes me,
> waiting for a discourse on *love*:
> San Michele where the monks prayed
> and their cells of strict observance,
> wave of radicals stuck to the city
> claiming God outside cloister
> walls.
> Only the columns remain.

---

* *Allusion to Gasparo Contarini, sixteenth-century Italian humanist.*

Murano

Gasparo Contarini prays in Santa Maria
Donato, Byzantine mosaics and fountain
lamps. Canals splash houses lightly
in morning and late night. Silence of
1500s monastic island. Reform,
radical observance return to poverty.

◆◆◆◆

Emperor dislikes God, no rival for
a despot, armies commanded to kill,
possess, level and empty. Destroyer
of sacred, mutilated prayers, abandoned
temples. To glorify yourself.
Enlightenment.

◆◆◆◆

Glass stretched like bubble gum,
blown sticky green gooey blue cotton
candy pink, necklaces and crosses,
carafes glasses flasks. Hanging colours,
sweet flowers, inviting tastes, chewed
and swallowed.

Cloaked in black, left to hang.

ONTOLOGY OF BLUE

Venice on a Monday

Murano where monks once
prayed, San Michele where
dead bodies are kept, walls
and underground, witnessed
by waves. White pearls turned blue,
and black. The angel left me alone,
the iron gates to the island locked.
Water splashed against
the island.

Sun spills into the lagoon
like pearls. A gondola rides
the waves, the gondolier tanned
by the Adriatic
wearing his white and blue
*camicetta.**

Cappuccino by the water, too
early for gelato,
cornetto with cream served
neatly in serviettes.
Papers spread news of lovers
and killers, politicians and thieves.

camicetta-t-shirt

DAVID BELLUSCI

Greedy pigeons compete
for bread crumbs, in piazza San
Marco, mothers with babies
in white, little boys in blue Italian
caps, dogs pulling ahead
on leashes. Souvenir trolleys
slowly uncovered, a morning
ritual. Delivery wheels pulled
on stairs, over bridges.

I watched Fra Angelico's angels
flap their wings, in blue red gold
take me from Santa Lucia
to white light of the Venetian
sky. Below the onion domes
bronze horses parade
in triumph. Steeples rise, watching
over the city with silent words.
A figure in a fluttering cape,
holds a bright torch
and leads the way.

SECTION 5

Purple fountains

ONTOLOGY OF BLUE

Montreal diner

    Smell of new binders, plastic
    crests, maroon college allegiance.
    Cars in three directions: Y-intersection.
    My eyes shut in rough traffic.
    "Mister Hotdog" ketchup and relish,
    campus route, fence after fence
    Victorian apartments my student res.
    A 2 a.m. bus our death sentence.

    Ripped dreamless by poisonous smiles,
    sharp razors to cut a lifelong curse.
    Her farewell hate-filled: to leave me
    in perpetual solitude. A mistake?
    A breeze carries her scent.
    Ice waters drown the cry of seagulls.

DAVID BELLUSCI

Cutting me

      The reaper declares his tools,
      the sickle to clear wheat fields
      and weeds. The victim before me
      stares, eyeballs rolling, sockets loose.
      My neck aching, I choke.
      The straitjacket is tightened
      parts of me surrender.
      Good crop to be kept,
      waste meant for the burning fire.
      The snipping starts, cutters in his hand:
      I watch the thrashing and pruning,
      not a manicured garden
      or abundant harvest, but hedges
      shaped, trimmed, hoed, and cleaned.
      The slicer skims across my neck,
      blades leave me skinned.
      I break free.

ONTOLOGY OF BLUE

Table for one

Snow on people's minds,
winter branches Christmas lights
waiting for white crystal magic shapes.
Jeanne Mince and Laurier, a scarf
too warm, coatless too cold.

Du Gascogne, cappuccino and French
chocolates. A mother with three
orders croissants and confecture
in French inflexions. Syllables
of children,
and a Japanese waitress.

In Paris the Eiffel Tower's silence
between us, her hand in mine.

Heart beats exchange, her lips glossy
red. Eyes betray our love story.

A dream her opium scent, swan-like moves.
Her breath, mine.

For one, please.

DAVID BELLUSCI

Unknown

Like a laser, sunlight hits the streets
months of grey clouds, rain lost

in whipped up dirty snow.

Swallow notes bounce leaves,
flies land in black crystal,
bees puffed yellow zigzag prints,
a Cessna hums far away.

Egocentric dandelions try
to hold hands, petals staring
at themselves. And I drink up
my dark Colombian incense
licking my blueberry fingers.

Crossing the street Jean-Paul Sartre
appears in nothingness
as I watch a middle-aged man,
green shirt and blue jeans exit
the aluminium framed grocery store.

Unknown to me, he is a person
without meaning.

Sartre whispers over my shoulder:
You, too.
Unknown.
Without meaning.

A squirrel jumps and stares at me.

ONTOLOGY OF BLUE

G.M. Hopkins on Friendship*

Where is the friend I'm waiting for,
close – far – here – here
I wonder I yearn I wish,
I don't see you in these forsaken times,
unkind unwanted unthankful,
another world, a universe unknown.
You wait. Will we meet? Soon!
You can admit
a friend's love you want too,
you demand, just as I do.
Together we'll live through rough times,
we shall live a-live live to-live just live.
You know my faults and strengths,
and you love me as I am, I ask for no more.
I hope. I believe. I'd like.
But I might not keep my promises.
You know my soul, what else counts?
Nothing really changes.
Nobody really changes.
Change is everywhere. Everybody.
A chance to change.
Change to chance.

You're good and pleasant, too.
You have values.
What attracts me to you is something
powerful:
> the Divine in you,
> that makes you,
> free to be you.

*Inspired by "What Art Thou Friend."

DAVID BELLUSCI

Unshaven

Chirpy, Sean's bushy chipmunk,
stretched out dead since eleven.
Country columns, a Victorian
porch, opens to massive oaks;
a road leads to town.
Her white and brown stripes
gold fur, barely visible in the dark.
She stares frozen at us.
Sean holds his glass, tilting,
ginger and rye, or Grand Marnier
to cap the night.
He's snug in his winter coat,
I'm wrapped in his grandma's quilt,
a slow scotch-drinker…
on ice.
Mosquitoes bite and suck their way
through flesh and blood,
keeping me awake.
Cars stop in front of the house,
Sean isn't sure why.
Not praying at the cemetery,
on the other side, the latest
tombstone a friend's suicide
– but looking here.
I doze off, as he lights another
Camel.

ONTOLOGY OF BLUE

> The clock ticks 3:30 a.m.,
> stands in front of me,
> I ask him if he's going to watch
> the sun rise again.
> He tells me no, staggers and sits.
> We hear the early morning songs,
> sky a lighter shade of blue, same star
> blinks over us.
>
> Let's go have breakfast.

DAVID BELLUSCI

Broken leash

Sit Sheba sit! Blonde hair covers
his rectangular office glasses
whiff of farm on his shirt.
She stares confused. She stands

tail wagging like a propeller
bites her leash steps neurotic
acts her mood. Master owner
unmoved. Tiptoes the walk.

Sheba forges ahead –
gets a good kick in the ribs.
Canine-tamer pulls her by the neck
like Caesar, dog's his business.

The bitch stares out – days, weekends
her ears up waiting to be rescued,
with her blonde master, or alone, in a daze.
Light cracks stained glass windows.
She breathes. A sigh. Whines.
Jealous of the hummingbird
she dreams of wings – flying.

Her tongue hangs, the door ajar
her Collie head pushes through
her tail up, darts as she schemed.

ONTOLOGY OF BLUE

She

      stretches freely under a cool
      cement bench stares at a fly
      buzz distracts her hummingbird's
      chirp startles her She observes.
      a sleek slender body tightens
      like a furry spring on two back
      paws She prepares her jump. bored.
      changes her mind. thick cream in
      the fridge She waits. I fill her
      simpson's cup about half-way –
      heavy rich cream. only her whiskers
      I see. her face buried She licks to
      the bottom stares around – at me
      the empty cup licking the taste
      – feline lips. She purrs her way
      to my bench along my back She rubs
      her head against my back and leg,
      closing and opening emerald eyes.

DAVID BELLUSCI

Two transfer

>Hugs her baby a surprise delivery.
>Licks his Vietnamese syllables
>rising-falling English, forms read
>checked signed in sweat.
>Strange letters unreadable words
>thanks for the Saigon baby seminar.
>A note, policy change
>she wipes her forehead.
>Spinning fans blow warm air on slow.
>Walls chipped bathroom blue squares,
>well-fenced crib.
>Baby eyes closed soft panda bear body
>moves into her arms – unknown woman,
>now his mamma.
>Half sleeping, tuft of black hair,
>she caresses him, he sucks his thumb.
>His little eyes open, a faint smile,
>unexepcted baby,
>tiny fingers closed,
>tenderness calms her, finding her love.
>
>Flight, buggy and house,
>   signing for hope ...

ONTOLOGY OF BLUE

Pretty woman

Night-time streets intersect
students pounding books
backpacks curving their bodies
lights flicker – the college campus.

Her red scooter, a bouncing woman,
checks streets, hands on front bars,
her handicap? A question. Young
at midnight, rides the dark.

Stares at sign blinking, she waits.
Drives her little machine
a bumpy road, black empty crisscross,
curly hair flips in rhythm.

Camaro cracks undisturbed night
passengers scream wildly
clanging bottles fill the car
a screeching driver, a sharp turn.

The scooter putters its own pace
straight, she drives
> not turning
> not noticing
> not caring.

Phone call

Both students, both 19, both at St. Pat's High. So, I thought, I should ask if they plan to marry, or was it too personal, but I did ask, and he said, he wasn't sure, but the girl had a hopeful expression that he would say, yes, after all, he was the father of the last baby boy, and then, he even had the father's Celtic blue eyes, but the older boy had the dark complexion of his Mexican father ... I picked up the phone at the first ring, her voice I recognised, but she sounded different – anxious – distraught, *he likes you,* she said, *I haven't told him yet,* she continued, *it's difficult, with all the complications I had with the last pregnancy, the infection, the C-section, the surgery, the bleeding. I almost died. I'm already showing. I can tell. I show right away. I just hope you'll be there for us ...*

ONTOLOGY OF BLUE

On the floor

      White smoke pipes across the floor
          la-la-la-la-la, ecstasy hair blows
pum-pum-pum
        floor moves, hard boots
stilettos her body her traces her mirrors
        la-la-la-la-la, steel poles
pum-pum-pum
sensuous shapes intoxicate
        arms rhythmic legs pulsate hips gyrate
        non-stop Bellini's
la-la-la-la-la, icy sweat,
pum-pum-pum
        his tight blue jeans,
faded,
silver buckle belt centres
        la-la-la-la-la leather gloves
pum-pum-pum
driving solo dancers,
        whistle – again– again – again,
la-la-la-la-la she turns returns overturns
pum-pum-pum
floor pounds she wears black lace
blood red lipstick, lips sync *chic … sweet*
        la-la-la-la-la dripping faces
pum-pum-pum

hairs stick throats dry heads spin
        magical dizzy knees hurt shirts wet
hard-finished floor bangs, she hangs on
tight to dry syllables
        la-la-la-la-la white smoke released
pum-pum-pum
tight space drinking drums, aching bones
        strings strum muscles pump
        pum-pum-pum…

ONTOLOGY OF BLUE

Portuguese dance

Townfolk from the islands, *Açores*,
*sopinha** opens Saturday night–
chicken or pork, mostly, and
oaky rosé *Mateus*, home-brew
dansar like the seventies colonies
lusophonia street mosaics.
Strings, *caxixi, berimbau*,
Rio, Lourenço Marques,
Lisboa – *senhoras** only please.
Mamma bends in red satin
fleshy daughter on her right arm,
sisters in Nevada blue jeans
and white blouses a tango flip,
grade school girlfriends
in black heels one last twirl,
no lambada tonight.
Church hall floor shakes
*sempre juntas** because it feels right
both secure in one move.
Shadowy shaven men exhale
sitting from plastic chairs
tapping shoes muscles tighten
yellow fingers and dry lips
hold back Player's:
break for the auction.

*sopinha** – *soup*
*senhoras** – *ladies*
*sempre juntas** – *always together*

Sleeping with Malebranche*

Amour seventeenth century,
fingertips press my lips,
undo my cotton shirt.
I drink the ocean,
answer to egrets.
A river silences me to sleep,
syllables of French aristocracy.
His collar tight, white pressed
folds into worn black. I want
to unloosen the stiff fabric,
help him breathe, wipe the dust
off leather-bound books on *vérité*.
His long fingers motion
his lips *venez ici*,
our evening stroll.
Moon, a watchman's night-lamp
hanging,
my heart wires of copper
my eyes switched on to know
Malebranche connects my soul:
Now touch the moon.

*Nicolas Malebranche, seventeenth-century French philosopher and priest.

Mornings in France

> *Cogito, ergo sum**
> "I think, therefore I am"

stretched out on embroidered sheets
across corners, I feel the mattress

half-asleep, half-awake,

crescendo mornings sing
and harmonize in ceaseless chimes

music of bells or birds, I wonder.

my desktop strewn – sheets of paper,
dry Bordeaux, works of Descartes

betray my evening passion.

light sneaks through quilted curtains,
inching … my hidden room

a forgotten village – southern France,

legs spread out,
my hands I fold, soft pillow

a breeze perfumes my nostrils,
humming flies, itching

sun warms my chest:

caressing touches I welcome,
delicately: lips – cheek – neck.

thick light and heavy warmth, I rise.

marching…trumpets…calling,
artist's impression brushed:

daylight imposes new day's painting,

white sheep weaving green hills,
blue-turquoise sky.

thoughts…I return to my notes, and write:

"I feel, therefore I am…"

---

*Philosophy of René Descartes (1596-1650).

ONTOLOGY OF BLUE

Morning hymn

Voices chant, pressed black suits and dresses,
foggy November, the sun withdraws,
morning hue coats the grass, I wait.

An open book, thick, pages flutter.
Glasses adjusted, he looks below the rim,
reads – slow syllables – stops.

The lady takes out her white handkerchief,
traces lace of her veil, perfect ponytail.
Holding his baby girl, the man rocks her.

Sacred words, ancient, fill the yard,
deeply dug ground, family plot,
ready to receive *the* earthly embrace.

Words stop, end of a concerto, book closed.
Soil sprinkled, empty space, a box lowered.
Man in the black robe makes a gesture.

Ground is filled, red and white roses thrown.
Boy lets go of his grandmother, walks over,
places an angel over the moist ground.

I watch the light rise.

The End...

The german shepherd choked on the bone and died.
The azalea was not watered and died.
The old lady stopped breathing and died.
The oncologist had cancer and died.
The pig was beaten and died.
The math teacher was hit by a car and died.
The farmer inhaled methane in the pit and died.
The X-boyfriend injected himself and died.
The blind lady tripped hit her head and died.
The black kitten was not fed and died.
The rat was poisoned and died.
The puppy dog was over-drugged and died.
The chicken bit a green mamba and died.
The star fell and died.
The river bed dried and died.
The bottle died.
The batteries to the electric shaver died.
The leader of the people's party lied and died.
The drive-through customer ate chicken nuggets and died.
The football coach shot his lover and died.
The trapped coyote bled and died.
The veteran was ejected from the roller coaster and died.
The priestess said the boy's funeral and died.

November leaves

> She removes wet flowers
> from her bag, purse on the ground,
> flowers in the glass vase.
>
> Kneeling, she doesn't hear
> the leaves crackle under her leather
> boots.
>
> She arranges white ... green,
> circles ... corners,
> opening rose petals, one by one.
>
> Her black coat dragging
> beneath her, a gold cross dropping
> over her blouse.
>
> Eyes count only roses, filling
> the vase, spreading green leaves,
> now in water,
>
> placed
>
> serenely below the picture
> of her father.

DAVID BELLUSCI

Plastic daffodils

>Grey stones lie in rows, angels spread wings,
>Names – a Cross – Mother Mary. I walk
>unknown, a place of peace RIP on each tomb.
>
>A flower pot of plastic daffodils
>dirty yellow rain earth, and dead flowers
>decompose beneath the family name.
>
>The person points upwards, a marble
>statue of a man or woman long hair
>and white robe, a reminder,
>
>*Heaven waits.*
>or *Judgment?*
>
>Names end in vowels or consonants,
>gather in words they know, shared, united
>in memories pronounced with beads and kerchiefs.
>
>Barren trees stand as columns, as though
>staring down bewildered, human fragility,
>finite losses. Footsteps heavy.
>
>Conversations repeated, no end in sight
>except November's scattered leaves.
>Cloaked sun withdraws, sky turns black
>
>cemetery lights die.

Alone

        Black dresses, black suits,
        black ties, black shirts, black
        sunglasses, black nylons, black
        shoes, black veils,
        red flowers.
        Before us she stands,
        her sonorous words in English,
        her words, his words,
        language, his language,
        a white kerchief, a little girl
        in white. They process.
        A train of black lace, tears
        in lace, a woman alone,
        her husband, her companion,
        she watches, lowered
        into the waiting earth.
        No children, only
        nieces, nephews, a sister.
        The man beside her when she woke
        now swallowed by merciless ground.
        She stares, wanting
        to believe, her grief can be expelled
        in a shriek crying out –
        disbelief she is alone.
        Holds her cane, calls his name,
        looks over, bending to see him below
        if only once again.

Gold box

Hershey's box hidden in the desk drawer
Saint Francis feeds the pigeons
postcard in Italian. I memorised the Canticle
chanted to a friend secretly under a bridge
in France when it started to rain in October.

Greetings from sister, signing her name
five children plus husband still finds time
care packages even to Amex in Cameroon.
She creates dishes – ingredients all Italian,
washes heavy pots and still runs a business.

I met Emily at university her elegant suit
jacket and skirt, a cameo initial her name.
Sunday morning coffee – the student cafeteria.
A series of thick letters her heart she explains
why she joined cloistered nuns in Kenya.

A cartoon *Miami Exit East* but the map
shows a car in Brazil. A couple lost.
We visited *Foz do Iguaçu* laughing,
crossing the border, we sang in a taxi:
I'll wash my socks in Argentina,
to the refrain: *You must be loaded.*

Familiar cursive writing not seen in years
birthday greetings, fifteen years back.
Weekly instalments of love tells her stories,
writing, an espresso, 5 a.m. her day starts.
Years without mom, life loses purpose.

They're fortifying the tower I occupy.
Told me to change rooms ... for the summer.

ONTOLOGY OF BLUE

Bruno

He stands curious at the glass entrance,
examines clouds, eyes lower set on longish grass,
like a puppy locked in. A restless repetition:
downstairs: window!
upstairs: window!
Yard waits, as if still waving. Grounds now
muddy, clouds loom large. He finishes
his coffee next morning, inspects ground, sky
from the side door:
clear blue green.

Bruno feels the starter, lawn mowers unknown
in his youth.
He pulls. Loose.
Hears the greasy motor. Smiles.
Hands tight. Motor revs.
Smell of grass cut he inhales and manoeuvres
around trees, mounds of earth.
His hockey hat on backwards, now betting
on Maple Leafs, Canucks eliminated.
Licks his parched lips,
humming motor delicious.

DAVID BELLUSCI

A Nun's Veil

>She secretly stares from the 8th story window
>steps back, her hand withdraws
>from the laced sheers. I wonder if many remain,
>never seen,
>just hidden.
>A brick museum adjacent, a chapel
>with precious saints a journey across
>the Atlantic reveals the foundress.
>
>A mission unveiled along the river shores, a port,
>teaching the inhabitants, a brick school their life.
>Settlement, colony, shaped in long black dresses
>and white trimming, fluttering in seasonal winds,
>moving on cobblestone roads,
>wet, smooth.
>Veils cover their ears,
>foreheads and neck,
>shapeless hips, ankles hidden.
>Huron children smile, the strange attire amuses.
>
>An inscription, a memorial, dotted
>with Spring tulips, planted by the orderly city.
>The restless river moves a song
>the same one as three hundred fifty years ago,
>when the mother superior arrived,
>
>the street bears her name.

ONTOLOGY OF BLUE

She stands

Nissans and BMWs race, speeding
around a traffic circle. She stands in her blue
Mantle, white dress, her hands

fold, eyes facing down,
smile, her gold crown regal.

Woman, *le culte*, spared by bulldozers
of New Order.

Meters away sellers, buyers strut
in black leather, XXX shop: *erotic delights*.
Red bras display, matching see-through
gowns.

Men stretch across wood floor,
muscles tracing torsos, yellow-green
underwear.

My eyes set on her from a distance
as though unseen, she stands
her face without blemish her dress
without scratch.

Glossy red Subarus, silver grey four-by-fours
rev the round-about.

License plates pretend:

je me souviens.

DAVID BELLUSCI

Standing in bronze*

        Iron solid in cloth folds,
        your cape pleats in motion
        the stars your audience.
        Beneath those layers, a scapular
        you betray your religion
        sheets of philosophy: monads
        one cosmic soul, infinite worlds
        mnemonics your hobby.
        Rector's rules you laugh at,
        you expose your god(s)
        Cicero's temples.
        That hood hides your eyes,
        but you peer down at me like
        an apocalyptic warning.
        The Book you hold here
        in *Campo dei Fiori*. What for?
        To remind us?
        Rome-Geneva-Paris-Oxford-Wittenberg.
        Obstinate teacher. Trouble-maker.
        You stand alone
        in the company of your eternal spirit
        the mob glares – at your naked youth
        prisoner's beard
        tightened neck
        silenced tongue
        tied.
        Fire burns.

*Burning of Giordano Bruno 1600.

ONTOLOGY OF BLUE

Chant

Cracking jokes, repainted walls
his off-white room, pictureless
replies, he sits upright.

Little boy seen in his brown eyes,
home country cabin, firewood,
well, slippery rocks, heavy furs.

Focussed *on what?* I wonder.
He sits alone – with all of us.

Few words – chosen – cautiously
selected in his reflection.

Ham and potatoes on his plate,
chipped cup with red hearts
he drinks water,
there-and-not-here …

Black hair razor-short, clean,
his nose, noble, eyes waiting
like a male virgin for his
fiancée.

Corridor calmness, looks down –
never up. He struts like a rapper
in white robes out-of-place in Latin
chants and ancient bricks.

Time in his room, an open book.

Duffel jacket and maroon knit hat
insulate him in icy snow,
rhythmic steps in both directions,
cloistered in barren trees.

I catch a guarded smile, so cautious,
he protects a secret.

He announced once –
he would defend me.

ONTOLOGY OF BLUE

Incense

>	Gloss spreads the waves
>	silk
>	hummingbirds break the silence
>	chipmunks utter chip sounds
>	cool mist, the breeze of
>	pine sprays
>	acorns crunch under my feet.
>	Standing, a row in white
>	cloth flutters like
>	processional flags
>	sweet words invite
>	morning's being and purpose.
>	And me.
>	Fingers move together, forehead to
>	chest, shoulder to shoulder.
>	The body inclines towards blue
>	heavens and the orange peaks of
>	light.
>	A voice clear syllables
>	advances into chant, series of tones
>	waiting a response.
>	Together, consonants, vowels
>	resonate.
>	A hymn, sacred verses,
>	birds watch,
>	their bodies bend.

Dedicated to a novice

    Finger signals, *complete the act,*
    you sigh at my morning
    fatigue and oversight,
    or sloppiness.
    Your belt hangs loose over your skinny
    body, even when you show me your
    fatty waist, I'm not convinced.
    I see your rib cage,
    white layers of bone.
    Army cut, your German-side,
    you parade your body as French.
    Your eyes neither blue nor brown, defying
    Saxons and Romans.
    Your chapped red lips
    move to Latin chants, I know you stole
    angelic chords. Your head
    bounces to Gregorian like your Rock
    days are not over.
    Your repeated *merci*
    and *is something bothering you,*
    words of your love.
    You echo Saint Thomas
    but you admit, a disciple of Plato. I
    understand. You suggest we have coffee,
    perhaps become "friends."
    My thoughts remain attached to duty –
    I love you most in prayer.